FUN FAX™

A[illegible]AL
[illegible]DOM

Written by Peter Lafferty
Illustrated by Mike Donnelly

HENDERSON
PUBLISHING PLC

THE ANIMAL WORLD

What is an animal?

Plants make their own food from air, water, and minerals in the soil.

Animals, on the other hand, do not make their own food. Instead, they eat plants, or other animals. They move around, too. Like all living things, animals reproduce (have babies).

There are at least one million kinds (species) of animals, ranging from tiny bacteria which can only be seen through a microscope, to the giant blue whale.

There are at least 700,000 species of insect, 11,000 species of birds, 5000 species of reptiles (snakes, lizards and their relatives), 13,000 species of fish, 3000 species of amphibians (animals that live on both water and land), 2000 species of centipedes, and 8000 millipedes. There are 35,000 species of arachnids - spiders and their relations.

Through the microscope

Most viruses, bacteria, yeasts and the spores of many types of simple plants and animals are too small to be seen with the unaided eye. Many hundreds of thousands of viruses could sit on the full stop point at the end of this sentence. Bacteria are on average 10 to 100 times larger than viruses, but few are larger than our own red blood cells (of which there are more than 5 million in each drop of blood).

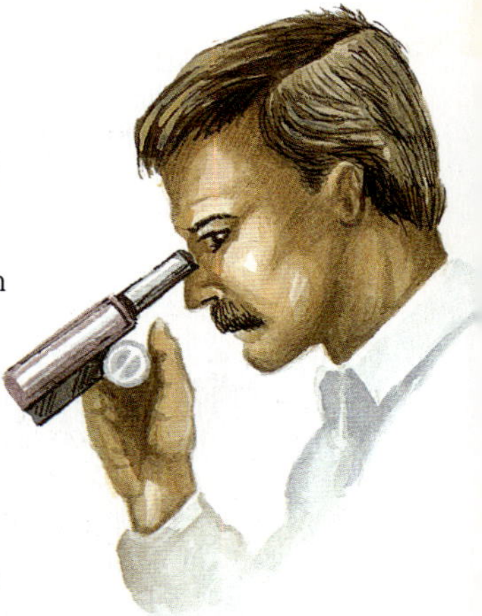

The largest animal

The blue whale is the largest and heaviest animal that has ever lived. It can grow up to 33m long and weigh around 200 tons, the weight of 40 elephants. The elephant is the largest land animal, but it only reaches a height of 3.5m. The tallest land animal is the giraffe which reaches 5.5m.

Most dangerous animal

The most dangerous animal is not the lion nor tiger, but the parasite, a microscopic animal which causes the disease *malaria*. This tiny creature has probably been responsible for more than half of all human deaths.

The largest jellyfish

The largest jellyfish have a body more than 1.8m across, with tentacles 36m long.

The largest ray

The devil ray measures up to 6m across. It moves through the water by flapping its side fins like wings. Sometimes they leap high into the air.

The strongest creature

Hercules or Rhinoceros beetles, which grow up to 16cm long and are among the largest of insects, can withstand 850 times their own weight placed on their backs. Human weightlifting records achieve no more than about twice one's body weight.

Fast flapping

A tiny midge can flap its wings at a speed of over 10,000 flaps each second.

Smallest insects

Two insects are among the smallest members of the entire animal kingdom. They are the hairy-winged beetle and the battledore-wing fairy fly. They are only 0.2mm long. (The largest insect is the female giant stick insect which is 330mm long!)

Largest spiders

The largest spiders are the bird-eating spiders of South America. Their body can be over 7.6cm long, and their leg span more than 25cm. The smallest spiders, found in Australia, have a body less than 1mm long.

Smallest mammals

The smallest mammal (an animal that gives birth to live young which it feeds on milk) is Savi's pygmy shrew, which has a head and body length of 3.8cm. It weighs 1.5g. Pygmy shrews eat spiders and insects almost as large as themselves!

Most dangerous bats

The most dangerous bats are the blood-sucking vampire bats of tropical America. The bats are dangerous because they transmit diseases such as rabies.

Deep dives

Seals can dive to depths of over 1200m and stay submerged for two hours. They regularly dive down to 820m and when they surface are not 'out of breath'.

Many feathers

A bird such as a swan has 25,000 feathers.

Fastest animal

The peregrine falcon is the world's fastest animal. In a steep dive, it reaches a speed of 347km/h.

Slowest bird

The slowest flying bird is the American woodcock which can fly at 8.5km/h without sinking - but only during courtship displays. And at least half the world's flying birds can exceed an air speed of 65km/h in level flight.

The greatest traveller

The Arctic tern migrates every year from the Arctic to the Antarctic and back, a round trip of 36,000 km.

Largest wingspan

The largest wingspan of any living animal is that of the wandering albatross. It averages almost 3.2m, but is reported to reach over 3.9m. Bats have wingspans up to 1.8m, and butterflies up to 27.5cm.

Most abundant bird

There are at least 1,500 million red-billed quelea birds in the dry parts of Africa, south of the Sahara. At least 1000 million of the birds are killed each year to keep the population down, but with little effect. One colony was estimated to contain 23 million birds.

Smallest bird

The smallest bird in the world is the bee hummingbird of Cuba. Its body is just over 25mm long, and it is lighter than some moths.

Largest reptile

The saltwater crocodile of south-east Asia, Malaya, Indonesia and northern Australia is the largest reptile. Males may reach 4.8m in length and weigh over 500kg.

Largest lizard

The largest lizard is the Komodo dragon found on a few Indonesian islands. It can grow to over 3m and weigh 160kg. The longest lizard is the Salvadorian monitor of Papua New Guinea which can be over 4.75m long.

Most poisonous animal

The most deadly poison known comes from the skin of the golden arrow-poison frog of Columbia. An adult frog contains enough poison to kill 1500 people. Strangely, the deadly frog is preyed upon by a snake which is immune to the poison.

Weighing up worms

The longest earthworm ever found measured 6.7m in length. It was found in South Africa. The shortest worm is only 0.5mm long. The largest tapeworm is the human tapeworm, which may be up to 18m long. Specimens of 9m are common.

Largest centipede

The largest centipede is the Giant scolopender of central America which can grow up to 30cm long and is 2.5cm across. It is large enough to capture mice and lizards.

The largest and oldest amphibian

The Japanese giant salamander is the largest amphibian, growing up to 1.5m long. These creatures live up to 60 years in captivity, making them the longest-lived amphibian.

Largest meal

The largest meal eaten by a snake is probably a 91kg bear which was once swallowed by a reticulated python.

Many types of insect

There are about three times as many species (types) of insect as of all other kinds of animal put together. So far about 700,000 species have been described and named, but there are probably five times as many awaiting naming.

Many insects

It is estimated that there are around 10 million billion individual insects alive at any one time. For every human being alive, there are about a million insects - and a million insects would weigh 12 times more than the average adult.

Magnetic ants

Compass termites from northern Australia always build their mounds pointing north, possibly using the Earth's magnetism to help them find the right direction. Their mounds can be as much as 6m high, and take eight years to build.

Farmer ants

The leaf-cutter ant of South America grows mushrooms. They cut up leaves and plants into small chunks and carry the chunks back to their nest. Then they chew the leaves to form a compost which they spread on the nest floor. A fungus or type of mushroom grows on the compost, and the ants eat the mushrooms.

Brainy ants

The animal with the biggest brain in relation to its body is the ant.

Rancher ants

Ants keep herds of insects, called aphids, like humans keep cattle. The ants gather the aphids into their nests where they feed and care for them. When they want a drink, the ants stroke the aphids with their feelers and 'milk' them for a sweet liquid called honeydew.

Underwater dragonfly

The dragonfly spends most of its life underwater. The young dragonfly (larva) changes its skin several times as it develops underwater before it climbs up a grass stalk and emerges as a fully grown dragonfly. A dragonfly may live for several months. Some dragonflies can reach speeds of 64 km/h.

Dotty ladybirds

Different kinds of ladybirds have different numbers of spots. Some have one spot on each wing case. Some have 3, 4, 6, 7, 10 or 22 spots. Most have red wing cases with black spots, but some have black wings with red spots, and some have yellow wings with black spots.

Shell home

The young caddis fly (larvae) live in ponds and lakes. To protect itself, the larva builds a house of small pebbles and shells around its body, glued together by a sticky liquid from its body. Some carry their home around with them. Others attach it to a stone and live inside.

The sacred dung beetle

The scarab, or dung beetle, has a clever way of making sure that its young have something to eat when they emerge from its eggs. The beetle rolls a ball of dung into a safe hollow and lays its eggs inside the dung ball.

The ancient Egyptians thought that the scarab beetle was sacred and wore good luck charms in the shape of the beetle.

Cold light

The most efficient light source in the world is the glow-worm and firefly. Most light sources produce a lot of waste heat as well as light. But glow-worms and fireflies produce light without heat - cold light. A glow-worm makes 20 times more light from a given amount of energy than an electric light bulb does. The light is used to attract other glow-worms and fireflies for breeding.

The most legs

Millipedes have upwards of 200 legs, with the record being 710. Centipedes have between 28 and 354 legs. They can walk at speeds of up to 1.8 kph. They are unable to run. The next leggiest creature is the velvet worm, with up to 82 legs.

Dangerous prayers

There are about 800 species of praying mantis. They get their name from the way they hold their long legs folded in front of them, as if praying. But, they are not praying - they are waiting to seize their next victim. A female praying mantis is so dangerous to other insects, she will even eat her mate.

Champion jumper

Fleas can jump up to 350 times their own length. This is equivalent to a person making a long jump of over 600m. A person who could jump as well as a flea would be able to jump to a height of 260m.

Moths and butterflies

Moths and butterflies are different in several ways. One difference lies in their antennae. Butterfly antennae have knobs at the ends, whereas moth antennae are feather-shaped. Another difference is that, when resting, butterflies usually close their wings together, holding them straight up from their backs. Moths, on the other hand, fold their wings along their body.

Silken thread

The silkworm caterpillar spins a silken cocoon around its body to keep itself safe while it develops into a silk moth. One cocoon contains a thread of silk more than 1600m long. The silk moth caterpillar was bred for thousands of years by the Chinese for its silk.

Migrating butterfly

The monarch butterfly spends its winter in the Gulf of Mexico and migrates to Canada in the spring. Along the way, the monarch lays eggs which hatch and carry on the journey. In Europe, the painted lady butterfly migrates between Iceland and north Africa.

Sleepy cicadas

There are around 2000 species of cicadas, insects that make a shrill clicking noise on hot evenings. The periodical cicada burrows into the ground as soon as it is born. It finds a nourishing root and feeds upon it, almost asleep, for 17 years. Then it wakes up. It crawls to the surface and appears as a full-grown cicada. For five weeks, it enjoys a normal cicada life, then it dies. Another species lies underground for 13 years.

The ant that eats itself

The queen of the black garden ant feeds partly on its own body. After mating in midair during the summer, the queen returns to the nest and bites off its wings for food. She relies on this source of food and her body fat to survive until her eggs hatch and the newborn worker ants can feed her.

Short-lived mayfly

The shortest-lived insects are mayflies. They often live only for four or five hours, or at most for a few days. The longest-lived insect is the termite queen which can live for 20 years. Most insects live, as an adult, for a few weeks.

Seeing without eyes

Some insects, such as cockroaches, respond to light even when all their eyes are covered. Some cockroaches will avoid light even if their head is cut off. These insects seem to have light-sensitive skin.

Hearing with the legs

In some crickets, the ears are on the animals' legs. They consist of drum skin-like patches of skin overlying sensory cells. They are sensitive to high-frequency sounds. A male cricket uses its ears to home in on the female's chirps.

A plague of locusts

A swarm of locusts (type of grasshopper) can be more than 50km long and 8km wide. It might contain 500,000 million insects. Such a huge band of hungry insects can eat the food needed by 20 million people.

Millions and millions

A female cod fish may lay more than 6 million eggs during each breeding season. Sometimes several hundred thousand eggs are laid in a day. But on average only one or two eggs will grow into adult fishes. Most are eaten by other sea creatures. To compensate for this high rate of loss, most fish lay a huge number of eggs.

Electric fish

There are several fish which can give an electric shock to anything which touches them. The electric eel of South America can grow to 3m long and produce enough electricity to stun a horse. It easily stuns small frogs and fish which it then eats. The electric catfish of Africa is half the size of the electric eel but is almost as deadly.

The archer fish

The archer fish of southeast Asia shoots down its prey with a jet of water. It can hit insects about one metre away with a vicious squirt of water from its mouth.

The four-eyed fish

In tropical America, there is a fish with four eyes. This strange animal swims on the surface of the water, searching for insects to eat. Its eyes are half in, and half out, of the water. The upper half of each eye is adapted for seeing in air, and the lower half is adapted to see in water. So the fish can watch above and below the water at the same time.

Seagoing mammals

Whales spend all their lives in the sea, but they are not fishes. They are mammals; that is, they give birth to live young which they feed with their own milk.

Fish are cold-blooded; whales are warm-blooded. Their body is protected by a thick layer of fat. Fish can breathe underwater through their gills; whales breathe air and must come to the surface to breathe. Some types of whale can stay underwater for over an hour before needing a breath of fresh air.

The call of the whale

The call of the humpback whale is the loudest noise made by a living creature. It is louder than a supersonic aircraft taking off, and can be heard up to 800km away.

Sink or swim

Most fish have a bladder or bag of gas inside their bodies which allows them to keep afloat without effort. However, the shark family does not have this bladder (called the swim bladder) so they must keep swimming all the time. If they stopped swimming, they would sink to the bottom of the sea. Some members of the shark family have given up the struggle to keep on the move. They are the rays, which spend their time lying on the sea bed, eating shellfish and other food found there.

Shark's teeth

The shark is perhaps the most deadly predator. Expect no mercy from an attacking shark. Attacking sharks may become so frenzied that they eat themselves. They seem to feel little pain. A shark may have up to 1000 razor-sharp teeth. The teeth are arranged in a dozen or more rows. The teeth gradually move forward as the front row wears out.

Jet propulsion

The squid moves by jet propulsion. It forces water backwards through holes in its body; the reaction to this jet of water thrusts the animal forward. One type of squid can even fly across the surface of the water like a jet plane.

Deadly stings

The Portuguese man-of-war is a poisonous type of jellyfish. It floats on the surface of the sea carried along by the wind and currents. It has a gas-filled bag which acts as a sail, catching the wind. Below the sea surface are trailing stings, up to 50m long. These stings can paralyse any fish that they touch. They can even kill humans.

Horse fish

The seahorse is a fish with the head of a horse and the tail of a monkey. It swims upright using a fin on its back and can move backwards, forwards, up and down. It curls its tail around a stalk of seaweed to stay still. If danger threatens, the seahorse can change colour to blend into its surroundings. One unusual thing is that the male seahorse give birth to the young. After the female has laid her eggs, the male keeps them in a pouch until they hatch.

Cut away

The sawfish is a type of shark. It grows about 8m long. On the front of its head is a saw-like blade with sharp teeth on each side. The blade can be up to 2m long. The sawfish uses the blade to scrape food off the sea bed, and to stun its prey. The sawfish dives into a shoal of fish, lashing its blade from side to side.

Deadly delicacy

The puffer fish is one of the most poisonous creatures in the world. A few mouthfuls of its flesh is enough to poison any creature that tries to eat it. Except in Japan, where the puffer fish is regarded as a great delicacy! Japanese cooks are specially trained to cook the puffer fish in a way that neutralises the poisons. However, if the cook is not an expert, the customer is likely to die.

Man eater

The grouper is one of the largest bony fishes found in warm seas. Some groupers weigh up to 4500kg, the weight of an elephant. These large fish are fearless and attack anything that approaches their territory. There are many stories of groupers attacking and killing human divers.

Blood pipes

The blood vessels of a blue whale are so large that a full-sized fish - a herring or trout - could easily swim through them. The largest blood vessel in the human body, the aorta, is about 2.5cm in diameter.

The biggest eyes

The largest animal eyes are those of the giant squid. Each measures 40cm across and contains more than 1,000 million light-sensitive cells (nearly 100 times more than our own eyes). These cannot distinguish colours, though. So whilst a squid sees as well as we do, it is only in black and white.

Heart or head?

A shrimp's heart is in its head.

Hearing without ears

Most fish have sense organs spread over the body which detect pressure waves in water. The organs form a network along the sides and on the head of fish known as the lateral line. Fish use this to detect movements in the water and so help them avoid objects.

Flying fish

Flying fish leap into the air, from the surface of the water, at speeds of 32 km/h. A flick of their tails gets them airborne and if they fall back into the water, another flick lifts them again. They have been known to soar 6m into the air and glide along for a distance of 400m.

Fossil fish

For many years, a fish called the coelacanth was thought by scientists to be extinct. But in 1938, a 1.5m specimen was caught off south Africa. Since then nearly 100 specimens of this unique fish have been caught near the Comoro Islands off Madagascar. The coelacanth has strong fins which it could use as legs. From their relatives evolved the first land animals.

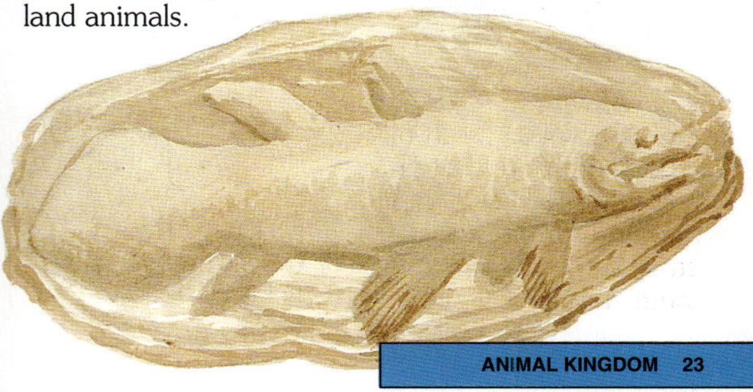

BIRDS AND OTHER FLYING CREATURES

House-proud bird

The bowerbird comes from New Guinea and Australia. The male bowerbird makes a dancing area out of twigs, surrounded by walls of upright sticks which curve over the top. It then places coloured feathers, stones, and any brightly coloured object it can find on the floor to attract the female.

Greedy bird

Unlike the pelican, a puffin does not have a pouch beneath its beak to carry food. Nevertheless, a puffin can carry up to ten fish at once in its beak. The bird carefully arranges the fish lying across its beak, with all the heads on one side and all the tails on the other.

A living nest

A king penguin does not make a nest to house its young. There is nothing to make a nest from in the cold Antarctic waste where the king penguin lives. Instead, the egg is kept warm between the legs of the penguin, resting on the feet. When the egg is hatched, the young penguin is protected from the cold in the same way.

Penguin high jumper

The Adélie penguin spends most of its time in the cold Antarctic waters. They travel more than 800km each year between their feeding and breeding grounds. Although they are awkward on land, they swim well. When they arrive at their destination, they jump straight out of the water up the steep sides of an ice flow. They can jump three or four times their own height.

Long tongue

Woodpeckers have very long tongues. They use their tongues to pick insects out of cracks and holes in trees. These birds are very well adapted for climbing and drilling into the trunks of trees. They have two toes pointing backwards and two pointing forwards to help them grip the tree trunk. Their short, stiff tail is used to support their weight when climbing. Their strong, sharp beak is ideal for boring holes into bark and wood. The woodpecker's beak strikes a tree at a speed of 21km/h.

Smelly nest

The nest of a kingfisher smells dreadful. It is a small chamber at the end of a narrow tunnel in a river bank. The young kingfishers live in the nest and are fed on fish. The nest soon becomes full of fish bones and bits of rotting fish. Most birds clean their nests of waste but the kingfisher does not. On a hot day, the droppings and rotting fish makes the kingfisher's the smelliest of all birds' nests.

Martha, the last passenger pigeon

In the early 1800s, the passenger pigeon was very common in North America. Huge flocks of up to 2000 million were seen, stretching for almost 324km. But the pigeons were slaughtered for their meat. By 1900, there were only a few passenger pigeons left, in zoos. The last passenger pigeon, called Martha, died in Cincinnati Zoo.

Bird babysitting

The wandering albatross holds the record for the longest normal incubation period. It sits on its eggs for around 80 days. The shortest incubation is that of the great spotted woodpecker and the black-billed cuckoo. These birds hatch their eggs in 10 days.

Big egg

The kiwi is a small, rare bird which lives in New Zealand. Its egg is almost one quarter of the bird's body weight - very large for such a small bird. The largest egg is the ostrich egg which is up to 20cm long. You could feed twenty four people on the omelette made from a single ostrich egg. It would take about 40 minutes to boil an ostrich egg.

Bird hitchhiker

One type of bee-eater hitches a ride on the back of larger birds, such as storks, as they walk along the ground. The small bee-eater catches grasshoppers and other insects that are disturbed by the stork's feet. Other types of bee-eaters catch bees, wasps and dragonflies as they fly through the air. Before they eat the insect, the bird rubs the insect on a branch to get rid of any poisons in the insect's body.

The butcherbird

The shrike, or butcherbird, hunts mice and lizards and small birds. When they have caught some food, the shrike hangs it on sharp thorns. This is because the shrike does not have strong claws and finds it difficult to tear flesh from the prey, without the help of its 'butcher's hook'.

Fast flapping

A hummingbird can flap its wings 90 times a second. This is so fast that a 'humming' sound is produced. The fast flapping means that the birds can control their flight perfectly. They can hover and fly backwards as their long tongue probes into flowers to drink nectar.

Head in the sand?

Ostriches do not bury their heads in the sand when frightened or alarmed. Instead, they crouch down and their dusty colouring makes them almost invisible. They can fight fiercely when attacked, delivering a powerful kick with their legs. They can also run away from danger - at speeds up to 65km/h.

Hungry bird

The blue tit must find between 500 and 1,000 caterpillars each day to feed its brood. When nesting close to woodland, the hen will lay up to 14 eggs, but in gardens where food is scarce smaller clutches are normal.

Flying forever

The sooty tern can fly for up to four years without landing. It feeds and sleeps on the wing.

Flying without wings

The bat does not have wings, yet it can fly. It has a membrane, or skin, stretched between its elongated fingers and between its arm, body and leg. When the bat flaps its arms, they lift the animal as if they were wings.

The flying squirrel also has skin flaps between its arms, body and legs. It uses these to glide from one tree to a lower one. Bats and flying squirrels are not birds, but mammals. They give birth to live young and feed them on their milk.

Finding the way in total darkness

Bats do not use their eyes to find their way about or to catch their prey. For one thing, they live in dark caves and hunt during the night. Instead, they use sound to find their way. They emit very high-pitched (ultrasonic) squeaks as they fly. The echoes of these sounds are used by the bat to navigate. Vampire bats can hear sound with frequencies over eight times higher than any picked up by human ears. The Rousettus fruit bat can locate objects only 0.5mm across while flying at top speed.

The fishing bat

In Mexico, there is a bat that catches fish. It flies close to the surface of a stream, dangling its legs into the water. Fish near the surface are caught in its claws.

Largest and smallest bats

The largest bat is the kalong, or Malayan greater fruit bat, which has wing span of up to 1.5m, and weighs about 1.9kg. It is also called the flying fox. The smallest bat is the bumblebee bat which lives in Thailand. It has a wing span of 16cm and weighs only 1.75g.

All different

Tortoises, terrapins and turtles are all different. Tortoises live on land and have short, stubby legs. They tend to be small but can grow into giants, such as those found on the Galapagos Islands. Turtles live in the sea. They have legs like flippers. Terrapins are small and live in fresh water. They have slightly webbed feet.

Crocodile creche

The Nile crocodile lays her eggs well away from water and covers them with sand. When the eggs are about to hatch, the mother will hear the crying of the babies within the eggs. She uncovers the eggs so that the babies can break out. Then she carries the young in her mouth, down to the water's edge.
They swim in safe 'nursery areas' until they can look after themselves.

Gentle dental care

The crocodile is a vicious killer. Yet it lets a bird called the plover into its mouth and does not harm the small bird. The plover is the crocodile's dentist. It picks pieces of decaying food from the crocodile's teeth. Scientists call this behaviour 'symbiosis', which means 'living together'. There are many examples of animals helping each other. For example, the oxpecker picks ticks off the buffalo's hide, and makes its home on the buffalo's back.

Alligators and crocodiles

Alligators and crocodiles are very different. Alligators are heavier and slower than crocodiles.
An alligator's snout has a rounded shape. The snout of a crocodile is more pointed and turned up at the front.
Crocodiles have fewer teeth than alligators. They have a large tooth which protrudes from their lower jaw when the mouth is closed. This cannot be seen when an alligator closes its mouth. Alligators are only found in the Americas, except for a small Chinese alligator. Crocodiles are found in America, Africa, Asia and Australia.

Frogs and toads

Frogs and toads look alike but are different in a number of ways. Frogs have smooth shiny bodies and long back legs. Toads have a dry skin, covered in warts, and short legs. Frogs lay their eggs in large masses which float on the surface of ponds. Toads lay their eggs in long strands which are attached to underwater plants.

Hungry father

There is a frog in Chile which swallows its young. The male frog waits by the eggs until the young are about to hatch. He then swallows the eggs. The eggs fall into a large sac that hangs beneath his body. Here they remain until they grow into tiny young frogs. Then the father spits the young frogs out and they swim away.

A pocketful of eggs

The pipa frog has an unusual way of looking after its young. After mating, the male pushes the eggs onto the female's back. They stick there and skin grows around them. The eggs are completely safe in a pocket of skin. Within two weeks, tiny tadpoles can be seen moving around under the skin. After another week, they break out of their pockets and swim away.

Tongueless toads

In South America and Africa, there are toads with no tongues. They live completely underwater and have no use for a tongue. They have sensitive fingers which they use to feel their way through the murky streams where they live. The tongueless toads of Africa are called clawed toads because they have a claw-like point on the top of their fingers.

The goliath frog

The largest frog in the world is the goliath frog, found in west Africa. It can grow as large as a small terrier dog. It feeds on crabs, snails and sometimes fish which it finds in the ponds near the Congo river.

Using your head

Some Mexican tree frogs use their heads to survive. They are called helmet frogs because they have bony bumps on the top of their heads. When a drought comes, the helmet frog crawls into a hole in a tree trunk. Once inside, the frog plugs the entrance with its head. The tough helmet protects the frogs and loses little water.

The flying frog

The flying frog has large webbed feet. When the frog leaps from a high tree, it spreads out its webbed feet and these act as small parachutes. This allows the frog to sail through the air for long distances.

Forever young

The axolotl is a salamander which lives in Mexico. It looks like a normal salamander except that it has feathery gills for breathing underwater. It is, in fact, a salamander that has never developed into a mature salamander. Throughout its life, it remains in its immature state and never grows up.

Out of the fire

It was once thought that the European fire salamander was born out of fire. This belief was fostered by the fact that the salamanders were often seen crawling out of burning logs. In reality, the creatures had been driven out from their hiding places under the bark by the heat and flames.

The monster lizard

The Gila monster lives in the deserts of Arizona, Utah and New Mexico. It grows to a length of about 60cm and becomes vicious when hungry or alarmed. It is one of the few lizards with a poisonous bite. The Gila monster can store food in its tail so that it has a food supply when fresh food is scarce. When its tail is full, the lizard looks tail-heavy and unbalanced.

Hard-of-hearing snake

There are around 2000 different species of snake in the world. None of them have proper ears. They cannot hear sounds, as we do. Instead, they sense the vibrations of the ground which pass through their bodies to a sensitive organ near their jaw. When a snake charmer pretends to sooth a snake with music, the snake cannot hear the music. The snake responds to the vibrations of the charmer's tapping foot.

Flying snake

In the forests of Borneo, there is a snake that can fly. It can glide for up to 20m through the air from tree to tree. It bunches itself up into an S shape, and flattens itself by spreading out its ribs. This allows it to catch the air as it falls and it can control the direction and length of its glide.

The big squeeze

Pythons, boas and anacondas, the largest of all snakes, kill their victims by squeezing them to death. These snakes wrap themselves around prey, then constrict (tighten their grip by contracting their muscles) until the victims suffocate. Then they eat their meals whole.

The effect of temperature

The sex of young turtles is determined by the temperature at which they develop. If the temperature in the nest is below 28°C, all the young will be males. If the temperature is above 33°C, all the eggs hatch into females. If the temperature is between 28 and 33 °C, roughly equal numbers of males and females will be hatched.

Whiptail ladies

One species of the whiptail lizards of the southwest United States consists of females only. The lizards reproduce by 'virgin birth'; no sex is involved. They lay unfertilised eggs which hatch into identical copies, or clones, of the parent.

Thirsty frog

There is only one frog, found in south America, that drinks water.

Looking after baby
Mammals are warm-blooded creatures. They keep the temperature of their body steady despite changes in the temperature around them. To help them do this, mammals are covered with hair or fur. Mammals also give birth to live young which they feed with their own milk. Most mammals retain the unborn young inside their body while they develop although a few mammals, called the monotremes, lay eggs like reptiles. Humans, cats, dogs, sheep, apes and monkeys are mammals. Whales and dolphins are marine mammals. The duck-billed platypus and the spiny anteater from Australia are the only monotremes.

Hairy beasts
All mammals have skin on the body, including whales and seals. On a human's body there are about 1 to 2 million hairs, with about 100,000 of these on the scalp. Each hair on the head grows up to 8mm in length per month, growing for about three years before being replaced by another.

Kinds of ape

Apes are bigger than monkeys and they do not have tails. There are four kinds of ape: the gorilla and chimpanzee from Africa, the orang-utan from Borneo and Sumatra and the gibbon from southeast Asia. The apes are closely related to humans. The chimpanzee is our closest relation in the animal world.

Noisy monkey

The loudest monkey of all is the howler monkey. When it screams, it can be heard 5km away. When a family of howler monkeys travel through the forest, the noise can be mistaken for a thunderstorm. These monkeys have a pouch under their throats which amplify (make stronger) their voices.

The ugliest monkey

The male proboscis monkey from Borneo has to be the ugliest monkey of all. It has a long, flabby nose which hangs over its mouth. As the monkey gets older, the nose gets longer and longer. Some proboscis monkeys have noses that hang 17cm below the mouth.

The secret language

The marmoset monkeys from central and south America are the smallest of all monkeys. One marmoset, called the pygmy marmoset, is only 15cm long. Marmosets talk to each other using high-pitched sounds that humans cannot hear. So when marmosets seem to be silent they may be using their secret language.

Hares and rabbits

Hares and rabbits are different. The ears of a hare are longer than a rabbit's ears and its hind legs are longer than its fore legs. The hare is also much bigger than a rabbit. Rabbits like to live in groups underground whereas hares like to live above ground, and not usually in groups.

March of death

The lemming is a small mouse-like creature that lives in the mountains between Sweden and Norway. Every four years or so, the lemmings go on a march of death. If there is too little food in one area, the lemmings move along ancient migration paths in search of food. They destroy anything in their way. Many die trying to cross rivers in their path. When the lemmings reach the coast, they plunge over cliffs into the sea and drown.

Long neck

A male giraffe stands at 6m from head to toe. Its tongue can stretch out about 45cm to pick leaves off tall trees. Its neck can be 2m long. However, there are only seven bones in a giraffe's neck; this is the same as in a human neck.

Flowery nose

A mole's hair stands straight on end so that it can fold down either way when the mole moves back and forth in the tunnels where it lives. In America, the star-nosed mole has a ring of twenty two feelers on the end of its nose, which look like the petals of a flower. The feelers are sensitive to touch and help the mole find food.

Useful tail

A squirrel can fall 30m without hurting itself. It uses its long bushy tail as a parachute, slowing its fall. The tail is useful in other ways, too. It is used for balancing when the squirrel leaps from branch to branch. In winter, the squirrel wraps its tail around itself as a blanket to keep warm.

Elephants' graveyard

Elephants are very sociable animals. They live in groups of up to 40 members, usually led by an adult female. Elephants try to help each other when they get into difficulty. A sick or injured elephant will be protected. If a sick elephant falls down, the others try to lift it up again. Some people believe that elephants have a special place where they go to die - the elephants' graveyard.

Slow sloth

The sloth, found in South American tropical forests, is the world's slowest animal. It travels at around two metres per minute. The sloth is also very lazy. It spends its time hanging upside down from a branch by its hooked claws. The sloth rarely bothers to clean itself and is often covered with green algae that grows in its fur. Its hair grows in the opposite direction from that of other mammals.

The big sleep

The North American woodchuck spends eight months of each year asleep. It is active only during the summer. Like all hibernating animals, the woodchuck eats more as the winter approaches, building up a layer of fat. When the fat has reached a certain level - about one-seventh of the animal's body weight - the woodchuck retreats to its burrow for the long winter.

Deadly enemies

The Indian mongoose and the snake are deadly enemies. The plucky mongoose will attack any snake it comes across, even the dangerous cobra. It relies on its speed, dodging the snake as it strikes. In some areas, the mongoose was introduced to help get rid of the snakes but the clever animals quickly found it was easier to catch chickens than snakes and so these schemes were not a success.

Dam builders

North American beavers are champion dam builders, constructing dams up to 66m long from hundreds of tree trunks. Even a small dam is 20m long. The beavers build their homes, called lodges, in the pond which builds up behind the dam. The lodge can be a large structure, 1.8m high and 6.5m across.

The size of an elephant

The largest elephant recorded stood about 3.8m high. The smallest elephant is the Pygmy elephant, a type of African elephant. The males are only about 2m high.

Fast breeders

It has been calculated that if there were no casualties, one pair of rabbits could have 13,718,000 descendants in three years. In Australia, there were no rabbits in 1800. By 1900, the descendants of a few pairs taken there by settlers had overrun the country.

Muscular ears

Dogs have 17 muscles in each ear. They are needed to lift the ear, lower it and swivel it.

The hungry shrew

A 2g shrew eats three times its own weight in food each day. This is the same as an adult man or woman eating 1 sheep, 50 chickens, 60 loaves of bread and 12 dozen apples.